# UN-LEASHED

PRACTICAL STEPS TO
GET YOUR LIFE UNSTUCK

MARIANNE CLYDE

Copyright © 2016 by Marianne Clyde

*Un-Leashed*
by Marianne Clyde

Printed in the United States of America

ISBN-13: 978-1533017703
ISBN-10: 1533017700

All rights reserved. No part of this document may be reproduced or transmitted in any form, by any means (electronic, photocopying, recording, or otherwise) without the written permission of the author.

# Table of Contents

Welcome ..................................................................... v

### Part 1
### Identifying the Problem

Chapter 1
    Where Am I Stuck?...................................................11

Chapter 2
    How Do I Get Unstuck?............................................19

Chapter 3
    How to Begin............................................................27

### Part 2
### How Meditation Gets Your Brain Unstuck

Chapter 4
    What Is Meditation Anyway?...................................35

Chapter 5
    It Does WHAT to My Brain?....................................39

## Part 3
## Developing a New Way of Thinking

Chapter 6
    Dropping Unhealthy Beliefs ........................................... 51

Chapter 7
    Yes, You DO Have Control ............................................ 59

## Part 4
## Mindfulness and Grounding Techniques

Chapter 8
    Getting Set Free ............................................................. 71

Chapter 9
    Getting Grounded ......................................................... 75

Chapter 10
    Getting Mindful ............................................................ 79

# Welcome

Sometimes it's just so hard to be in relationship with other people. They can be so irritating and annoying. They chew loudly. They leave their dishes in the sink without rinsing them off. They even put the toilet paper on the roll the wrong way! Geez. They can show up at the most inconvenient times and cause you to lose focus on what you were doing. The kids stay out late and send your mind swirling into a tizzy of worry. Then some jerk cuts you off in traffic, causing you to fly into a rage.

There are circumstances that create so much stress that they cause you to lash out at your kids. The economy threatens to force you to lose it all. It's certainly understandable that you feel scared or stuck or angry. Sometimes the pressure can just drive you to drink…or overeat…or have an affair…right? Sometimes it seems that the pressures of life threaten to make you crazy.

Certainly you've felt this way at one time or another. I know I have. I have found myself getting irritated, worried, angry, annoyed, disgusted. I have often thought, "Beam my up, Scotty," looking for an escape from the pressures of the moment. I have even mistakenly thought that it was someone else's fault that I was irritated or annoyed. Some people blame others for why they are angry or why they drink. Do you?

The truth is that we are deluding ourselves if we believe that. The truth is that we are our own worst enemy. As long as we are dependent on someone else to change who they are or what they do in order for us to be happy, we are chained to that person and his or her annoying patterns. If we are waiting for someone else to apologize in order for us to be released from our hurt or anger, we are chained to them for the rest of our lives. If we can't quit drinking or smoking or overeating until the world becomes a less stressful place, we are in for a long, bumpy ride that will kill us in the end. Will there be some sort of satisfaction we feel at the end of our lives as we lay dying from a heart attack or cancer, blaming our kids or our spouse or the economy?

What if we were the masters of our own fate? What if we were free? What if we had this beautiful set of wings that we didn't even know existed, that have been bound up by blame and deflection of responsibility?

What if we were no longer held captive by anger or hate or unforgiveness? What if we had the power to be set free from the chains that have kept us bound: little irritations, the judgments we make, the divisions that we have created? What if we could just detach from the drama and live our lives from a place of love and joy and peace? What if we could stop marinating in the slimy pool of negative emotions and limited beliefs? What if we could love ourselves enough and believe in ourselves enough that other people's opinions no longer left a scar? What if we discovered those wings? What if they could be released with a thought?

What would that look like? How would that feel?

It would look a lot like an **Un-Leashed Life**. And it would feel more amazing than you can even imagine.

Would you like to know how to get there? I have learned to live it and I am willing to share with you what I've learned. Come on. Let's learn to soar through this beautiful life together. Abundance and freedom are calling your name.

# Part 1

# Identifying the Problem

# Chapter 1

# Where Am I Stuck?

—⚏—

*Mindfulness*: The quality or state of **being conscious or aware** of something; a mental state achieved by focusing one's awareness on the present moment, while **calmly** acknowledging and **accepting** one's feelings, thoughts, and bodily sensations.

This bears repeating because there are very key concepts here.

*Mindfulness*: The quality or state of **being conscious or aware** of something; a mental state achieved by focusing one's awareness on the present moment, while **calmly** acknowledging and **accepting** one's feelings, thoughts, and bodily sensations.

The key elements that I want you to pay attention to here are:

1. The *state of being conscious or aware*, because most people are not generally practicing that state of being.
2. The next major concept is to *calmly accept* one's feelings, thoughts, and bodily sensations. The reason I want you to be aware of this is that most people resist or deny unwanted feelings, thoughts, or bodily sensations and think they have no control over any of this. If you are one of those people, my hope is that that will change before the end of Part One.

We are not stuffing or denying our feelings or thoughts. We are not pushing them down. We are not getting rid of "bad' feelings or thoughts. As a matter of fact, we are not judging them at all as good or bad. We are just acknowledging and accepting them for what they are. We are noticing them; we are validating them; and if we choose, we can then change them. You cannot change something that you don't know exists.

Some people think that living a life of mindfulness and meditation means that you push down and deny your negative feelings and try to come off like some kind of a saint. If this is what you are looking for, you won't find it here. Here we will learn to notice, to recognize, to acknowledge, and to respond to what is going on in this exact moment in a thoughtful, wise way. The way you feel, the way you are in relationships, where you are stuck, and why. And most importantly, how to change what you want to change and move in the direction you want to move.

Some of our primary troubles come because we refuse to acknowledge that something is even an issue. Our marriages fall apart because we refuse to address uncomfortable feelings. We suffer ill health because deep down underneath, we are harboring resentment that has become toxic to our bodies and manifests as physical disease. Very often healing comes when we begin to really be aware. When we let the uncomfortable stuff come to the surface, we can see it and then we can clean it up.

So let's bring the things that are keeping us stuck to the surface.

What is it you are struggling with?

- Is it uncontrollable anger that squeaks out when you least expect it? But you make it OK because "they deserved it" or "the guy's a jerk"?
- Is it a vague sense that something is wrong in a relationship but you don't mention it because you are afraid to make it worse? So day after day the relationship continues, becoming stagnant, boring, less intimate?
- Do you keep telling yourself that perhaps you should stop drinking because every time you do, you either don't feel well, you get injured, you get DUIs, or you get in a fight? But you tell yourself it's really OK because you should be able to control it; everybody else drinks and seems fine; maybe it's just your imagination?
- Are your clothes getting tighter and tighter and you keep condemning yourself for being so fat and over and over again you start a new diet or a new exercise plan; but then for some reason it only lasts a few weeks and you find yourself binging on something you've been denying yourself?
- Do you feel stuck in a dead-end job? Or one where you are jerked to and fro emotionally by a boss that you strongly suspect is a sociopath?

- Are your finances always coming up short? Your best intentions still can't seem to make them stretch and you get further and further in debt?
- Is there a fear that you just find debilitating? Flying in an airplane? Speaking in public? Going out of the house?
- Maybe you struggle with a feeling that you are ashamed of, but it's always there: jealousy, insecurity, self-consciousness.
- Or a way of relating to the world that just feels unhealthy and scary to you like anxiety or depression.
- Maybe you have a secret behavior that no one really knows about but it makes you feel awful or dirty or guilty. Porn addictions, gambling, shop lifting, or kleptomania?

Each of these situations comes from beliefs that you have that are not working for you. Keep in mind that this book offers some powerful tips and suggestions about how to change your thought patterns and behavior patterns, and it will clearly give you a place to start…a way of creating new thoughts and behaviors. And you can experience amazing results by just making a few changes.

However, if you make those changes and you still find you need individual help directly addressing your particular issues, please contact a therapist near to you to help you with your specific challenges.

But for right now I want you to take a minute…just one minute to identify and jot down the specific areas in which you feel stuck.

_____

_____

_____

*Where Am I Stuck?*

OK...Now that you have identified WHERE you are stuck, let's talk a little bit about what is keeping you stuck.

One little thing that might surprise you is that you are never upset for the reason you think you are. Sure, you might be thinking, well of course I'm upset because my spouse is being unreasonable. Or your boss is being a jerk. Or maybe you're upset because the traffic is bad.

Maybe you even feel that you overeat because it's the only comfort you have in life; maybe you've had an abusive childhood. Maybe you're depressed because you've endured a debilitating loss or have a terminal disease. Maybe you're anxious because you have a teacher who is impossible to please, or maybe you've just been that way your whole life and it's "just the way you are."

Maybe you drink because you came from an alcoholic family. Maybe you're stressed because you just don't have enough money. Perhaps you are depressed because you are single...OR maybe because you are in a bad marriage. Maybe you feel stuck because everybody else gets promoted ahead of you and you've been there longer.

Maybe people are rude to you. Maybe your schedule is too busy. Maybe your spouse is having an affair.

All those things seem like pretty good reasons to be upset or anxious or depressed...and they might be true.

BUT, they are not the real reason. Your spouse is not your problem. Your kids are not your problem. Neither is your boss, your pastor, or ISIS, or the Congress or God.

These things, as such, are things that you see as being outside of yourself. Outside your control. And very often that's why we think that they are the problem. However, if something outside of you has to change in order for you to eat healthy, or exercise, or feel happy with yourself, or stop being angry…if you have to retire or get a new job before you feel self-actualized, then chances are you will never feel fulfilled or happy or content in any circumstance.

But I am here to tell you that you can be happy today. Right now. The chains that seem to bind you can be broken as you sit there. Your journey to freedom and fulfillment has absolutely nothing to do with anyone or anything else. It has everything to do with you and with the way you view yourself, the world, and your very existence.

One woman that came to my counseling center said, "I was stuck on pause. Frozen in time. All forward motion in my life had ceased." Now that's stuck! Here's her story.

> *"I had been attacked and left for dead by my ex-husband of 20+ years. I had been in and out of therapy with posttraumatic stress disorder (PTSD), anxiety disorder, insomnia, and nightmares. I got through my days with Ativan, afraid to go to sleep and dream. My life was a 1,000-piece puzzle swirling around a wind tunnel, refusing to come together and make me whole again.*
>
> *Then I found Marianne.*
>
> *…I knew right away she was going to help me. I felt safe and encouraged to uncover everything to put the pieces together. I was able to remember a period in my childhood that was blank and disturbing. We put the puzzle together. My childhood started to make sense.*
>
> *I found answers.*
>
> *I found ground zero where it all began and took my life back.*

*I have been able to deal with any anxiety now without medication.*

*Sleep is returning. I have a new normal that I like very much.*

*I'm not frightened by the things that have happened to me anymore. We put the puzzle together and I feel a peace I haven't felt in a long time. Healing my physical wounds has been very straightforward. A logical predetermined order. Healing my heart and soul and the very essence of who I am has been a long journey. I never gave up and I eventually found Marianne. It's the first time I viewed therapy as having a beginning, middle, and end. I was able to say I'm done. I'm ready to take my new normal for a spin. With Marianne's help I feel like I'm finally the real me."*

Easy, right? In the next chapter we will talk about how to get unstuck.

## Chapter 2

# How Do I Get Unstuck?

Chances are that you are upset or stuck in a situation or a feeling because you have forgotten your true identity. You think others have control over you, over your joy, over your circumstances. They do not.

They like to THINK they do. But they are mistaken. The only reason you are stuck is because you think you are stuck. You do not know who you really are.

If you really understood how perfect and wonderful and powerful you really are, at your core, you would feel the chains falling off even as we speak. Let's talk a bit how you can recognize that truth.

One thing that is very common when we have a habit or a situation we want to change is that we focus on the very thing we dislike about ourselves. We focus on how much we smoke and how we'll never be able to quit. We focus on quitting drinking. We focus on our terrible marriage and how we have to get out of that. We focus on that overweight body we see in the mirror and think, *Ugh*.

We are focusing on the wrong things. Did you know that what you focus on increases? What you resist persists?

*This point was emphasized to me when I took a motorcycle class a while back. It was one of those weekend courses where you can get certified to get a motorcycle permit. I had ridden on the back of my husband's motorcycle for years but had never actually ridden one myself.*

*So each class member was given a little 250cc motorcycle, not too powerful, but powerful enough to learn the ropes. One of the key points to learning how to ride was to keep your eyes focused on where you want to go. If you want the bike to turn left, you need to be looking left; if you want to make a U-turn to the right, you need to look over your right shoulder. Easy. So as it turns out, we were doing an exercise in which we were learning how to make turns and follow a certain path.*

*The instructor was standing by one of the poles in the parking lot where we were supposed to bear left. I knew exactly what to do and I clearly understood the exercise. Yet as I started heading in the right direction, my focus was on the instructor and wanting to do everything right…so I kept looking at him. Then crap! I realized I was headed right toward him…Oh my God! I am going to hit the instructor! Geez! I am panicking, of course, and he calmly repeats (a few times), "Look in the direction you want to go…look left…look where you want to go" Finally I was able to take a deep breath and looked to the left, and lo and behold! I missed the instructor and was able to follow the course he had laid out! Whew! Simple concept.*

*Not easy, though, when you are in a mind lock that keeps saying,*

*"Don't hit the instructor...don't hit the instructor...don't hit the instructor."*

*As soon as I was able to get out of the mind lock, like magic, I missed him. I was very relieved, as you can guess...probably even more relieved that he was...but he never moved. He was confident that if I just did what he said he would be fine.*

Incidentally, I did ask him how many times he had actually been hit by a student on a bike over the years and he said, "Only twice." I was very glad I was not the third.

SO there you have it...a very real example of how important it is to focus on where you are going instead of where you DON'T want to go.

Let me just share with you a few more thoughts on how to get out of a "mind lock." We will spend a little more time on how to change your thinking later in the book. Granted, sometimes, it's difficult to do. We have years of thinking in a certain way under our belts and we think that we don't have any control over our thoughts, but that is not true.

Yes, thoughts come and go, but you don't have to believe them. You don't have to act on them or entertain them, allowing them to take over your life. It's just a matter of being conscious and learning to take control of your thoughts. This can happen gradually or quickly. In most cases it happens gradually.

Just understand that this is what your mind does: it thinks. That's just your mind doing its job. It's your job to learn to take control. Whenever you find yourself thinking a negative thought or focusing on how angry you are or what an idiot that guy was when he cut you off in traffic, all you have to do is take a deep breath and choose another thought: "He's probably in a hurry. I have probably done the same thing to someone else at some point. I choose to let it go. I purposely relax and release the anger." It's OK if you don't catch the thought right away. Just change the thought when you DO recognize that what you are thinking is keeping you stuck in anger, which you are choosing to release. As a matter of course, you will begin to recognize the stinkin' thinkin' sooner and sooner until the thoughts you choose become more habitually gentle. But you must be gentle with yourself; don't condemn yourself for not figuring it out sooner. Just praise yourself for figuring it out when you did.

Same thing if you find yourself obsessing about dieting and losing weight and condemning yourself. Take a deep breath and repeat, "I am whole, perfect and complete. I'm working toward my goals to get healthier, but I am already perfect and my body is following suit. I am healthier than yesterday; I am adopting healthier eating patterns. I love me and I'm taking care of me."

If you keep focusing on how fat you are and how you must lose those pounds, you will continue to yo-yo diet because you are focused on the pounds and the physical body that you are unhappy with at the moment rather than the real you and where you see yourself when you are healthy. Instead you must learn to focus on who you really are and what steps you need to take to unblock your natural flow of amazingness! Head in the direction you are going. Begin to move in truth. Focus on what things will look like once you are unstuck…how free will you feel? How powerful will you feel? Can you feel that joy?

I want you to take a minute and picture what things will be like for you when you have already begun to move in the new behavior or feeling. What does it feel like physically? What do you see? What do you hear? Where are you? What are you doing? Take just one minute so you can actually experience what the freedom feels like for you. So go ahead and try it.

* * *

Now that you have a little bit of a picture of where you are going...let's talk a bit about how to get there.

In my book, **Peaceful Parenting: 10 Essential Principles**, I address ten principles that are foundational to living a mindful, peaceful life and being a mindful, loving parent. What I want to talk about here is not necessarily the parenting, but the first three principles. They are foundational to everything I teach.

The first three principles from my book **Peaceful Parenting: 10 Essential Principles** are:

1. Connect with your creator.
2. Know your true identity.
3. Nurture awareness (mindfulness).

One of the most effective ways to calm the mind and increase physical health is to begin or maintain a regular meditation practice using these principles.

Many people practice a religion, yet in Western culture we think it's much more virtuous to be busy in that religion: To do good things. To pray by asking for things. To visit the sick. To feed the homeless.... These are all really good things and of course I encourage you to do them. But it's very important to get fueled up *first* through stillness and quiet meditation by plugging into your source, or connecting with your creator.

Doing good things is important, but if you try to do it from your own human strength you will burn out, get overloaded, or perhaps get caught up in competition or pride. You might end up going in a direction that is not really helpful or doing it for the wrong reasons.

A lot of people say that they don't have the time to fit one more thing into their schedule. The funny thing is that if you start your day connecting to the one who knows everything and understands what must happen to make your day efficient and successful, and let yourself just become one with that energy, you will be surprised at how efficient you can be and how much smoother things can go. It's your most important meeting of the day.

First things first: Connect with your creator by being still, listening, and absorbing who he is. Meditating.

Here is a definition of *meditation*:

Thinking deeply or focusing one's mind for a period of time.

There are many ways to do this. It can be done for religious or spiritual reasons or for relaxation or stress reduction. There have been many studies that show how mindfulness and meditation can actually change the brain and we will focus on those really interesting things in the next part of the book.

But for now, I want to give you a place to start and some suggestions for starting or maintaining your own meditation practice. Be aware that meditation and mindfulness are not the same thing but they are closely related. Meditation is a wonderful way to begin to live a mindful life, a life of awareness and stillness of spirit.

As a matter of fact, I am offering a FREE challenge on my websites. A 90-Day Happiness Challenge. You can check it out at either of my websites: www.marianneclyde.com or www.mommy-zen.com. When you sign up, you will be taken to a 25-question quiz where you can answer the questions and determine a "Happiness" score. Then you will be instructed to set aside 20 minutes twice a day or whatever time you can commit to meditate AND write down three things you are grateful for before you get out of bed in the morning and three things before you go to sleep at night. The challenge comes when you retake the test at the end of the 90 days and see your score increase!

# Chapter 3

# How to Begin

**Pointers for Successful and Easy Meditation Practice**

Find a comfortable, quiet place where you won't be disturbed.

Try to set a regular time in the morning and in the late afternoon and stick to it as best as you can. If you miss it one day, just resume your practice the next day. Be gentle with yourself.

Determine the length of time you want to spend meditating. I suggest 20 minutes twice daily.

If you need to use a timer, use one with a soft chime so you don't jolt back into reality.

I have studied several types of meditation: Primordial Sound Meditation, Transcendental Meditation. When I lived in Japan, I studied Zazen Meditation with a Buddhist monk who lived next door. I have practiced Japa Meditation as well as other types. I have read through the practices of some of the Christian mystics, searching for the most effective way to meditate, for over 20 years.

As you know, there are many different kinds of meditation. Here are the main points that I have gleaned:

Decide on a mantra or focus such as:

- A focus might be on your breath, in and out, feeling the cool air come in through your nostrils and leaving through your mouth. Notice how your diaphragm rises and falls when you are breathing deeply and effectively.
- Focus on the feel of your pulse or the blood moving through your hands.
- Choose a word or a verse. "I AM" is a good choice. Ahum is a way of sounding out the vibration in Sanskrit. Or you can use any name for God: Yahweh, Jehovah, God, Abba. Or you can choose a concept, like love or peace or compassion.
- OR just Ahhh or Ommmm. Or AUM. Concentrate on the vibrational quality as you repeat it slowly and silently. You may also do it aloud.

You WILL have stray thoughts. Count on it. Don't let it bother you. This is just you releasing stress and that's the point! When you notice that you are straying, just gently bring your focus back to your breath or mantra.

Do not look for any strange or weird spiritual experiences. Experiences may come and go, but if that's the reason you are doing it or you continue to focus on the experience you will miss the benefits of meditation.

Do not judge yourself on having a "good" or "bad" meditation. Just the fact that you sit there for 20 minutes out of the rat race, focusing on calming yourself, is all you need to have a beneficial experience. When you slow your thoughts down and draw inward, your brainwaves will slow down from Beta to Alpha. If you become very relaxed, you may even slip into Theta, a slower brainwave that usually happens in that place between waking and sleeping.

You will likely begin to see very subtle changes after a few weeks.

You may be wondering about the second principle I spoke about: "Know your true identity." Spending time in meditation, connecting to your creator, will lead you into the knowledge of who you really are.

When I connect with God or the creator or the universe, I ask myself, who is it that I am connecting with? He is love, joy, peace, patience, kindness, creativity, and wisdom. Always forward moving. Organized. Not affected by the opinions of anyone. He treats everyone the same. He doesn't bind up, he sets free. He is abundance. When I connect with him and realize that I am one with him, it makes sense to understand that I am also those things. My natural state of being is one of love, joy, peace, creativity, wisdom, and abundance. When I flow in those things is when I am most effective and happiest.

What I DO for a living is not who I am. I am all these things whether I am a therapist or a janitor or a mailman or president of the United States. It doesn't matter if I am a missionary or a businessman, married or single, white, black, Asian. It doesn't matter if I am a man or a woman or transgender. It doesn't matter if I am gay or straight. The truth is, we are all one with the creator of the universe and when we recognize that, we become rooted in him and our identity becomes established in all that he is. So, at our core, we are all perfectly created.

Yes, we have beliefs and behaviors that we don't like or want to change. Others have different personalities and may or may not agree with us. Just because we all have the same core doesn't mean that it manifests the same. We all are unique and special in our humanness.

There is not another like us. We are all on a journey and we must all figure it out in our own way. But we are connected and we are all love and joy and peace at the core and have the same access to that power. It begins to manifest in our lives as we begin to recognize it and live it out.

This life is a journey. It is not a destination. We don't just figure it all out and then rest on our laurels. We grow. As is evidenced in all of nature, if we stop growing, we are in the process of dying. So to judge another because they are not growing according to our plan or journeying in the same way that we are is totally counterproductive. Our only job on this earth is to become more of what we are created to be. Others cannot judge us because it's not their journey. No one else can evaluate if we are doing it right or wrong, because they are not us.

Most people spend more time judging others rather than working on building their own connection to the source of life; and if they do that and spend all their time being busy, working, doing, and not connecting, they will burn out. But that is not our business. Our business is to love, to live the joy that we are connected to. Our business is to create what we have been given to create. To work the plan we are given....

If we each can do this, then we can begin to live a mindful life. We can implement principle three, which is to nurture awareness. Be aware of how we are feeling, what we are thinking, embracing the present moment with the myriad of gifts it contains, and to live what we become aware of as we connect to our source. If we are living a mindful life and being aware of this present moment and embracing it with all of its beauty and challenges with grace, then we are living a full life.

Living a mindful life teaches us to live in this moment with all it has to offer without labeling it good of bad. It means not peering into the future, which is not possible anyway, and that creates anxiety and worry. Neither do we let our thoughts linger in the past for that creates longing for what was and we miss what is. Staying focused on the past creates sadness and grief, depression, and regret, and also keeps us from embracing this moment—which is in fact the only moment we have.

So this is why mindfulness is so important…it keeps us living our life to the fullest.

And this is why meditation is important. When you meditate, you are connecting to the source of all that is: love, joy, peace, creativity, wisdom, and abundance. Because you are marinating in those qualities, they will likely begin to manifest in your life. If you were to soak in a hot bath with Epson salts and lavender, toxins would be released from your body and you would have a lingering fragrance. This is what is happening spiritually.

**Summary**

So the principles that we addressed from my book, **Peaceful Parenting: 10 Essential Principles**, are:

1. Connect with your creator
2. Know your true identity
3. Nurture awareness

And, the three mindfulness principles that we went over in this chapter are:

1. Focusing and visualizing the successful outcome rather than focusing on the problem.
2. Establishing a lifestyle of gratitude.
3. Beginning and maintaining a regular meditation practice.

In **Part 2**, I will help you see what actually happens in the brain by regularly practicing mindfulness, gratitude, and a positive mind-set.

Now practice what you've learned and remember: Just breathe....

# Part 2

# How Meditation Gets Your Brain Unstuck

## Chapter 4

# What Is Meditation Anyway?

In this section we will talk about what meditation is and why I recommend developing a regular practice. We will also talk about how meditation actually changes your brain and what that can mean to you.

Keep practicing all three things we talked about in the last chapter and things will begin to change for you in some way. If you haven't started keeping a journal, it might be a good way to recognize and keep track of changes. Often they are subtle and happen in different ways than you'd expect. So many times we have in our mind the way things are "supposed" to turn out that we actually miss the miracle.

Did you practice visualizing and feeling how things will be for you when you are free from what is keeping you down? Remember that you are focusing on how you will FEEL when it is accomplished in you, not necessarily how it is going to happen.

For example, if your issue is that you are having trouble making ends meet and you want to have more money, you might be tempted to visualize getting a specific new job or having a certain person replace your current boss. You might be tempted to pray that you win the lottery or that a certain inheritance comes your way, and you could be very disappointed — even angry — if things don't turn out that way.

One thing that is very important about learning to live life on purpose is to humbly accept that when you are planning on change, you don't have to plan it out by the tiniest detail. When you live a life of mindfulness and meditation, you become aware that you are one with the very creator, the force that knows all things, the one who created all of this from nothing. He certainly knows how to guide you in and out of situations and to the best course of action for you.

It's kind of like a waltz. If you are dancing with a partner, you must let one of you lead and the other of you must follow, or you will step on each other's toes and stumble around and maybe even quit dancing because it's not fun anymore. On the other hand, if you've ever watched how magnificently graceful it is when the partners are working in tandem, one leading and one following, the beauty and oneness of the result is breathtaking.

If you want a positive result, let go of the need to control the process and outcome. Just visualize yourself already there and enjoy the ride.

It's actually quite amazing that as you begin to live mindfully, you become aware of how you feel, what's happening in your environment, being aware of the energy you pick up from others, watching and catching your thoughts before they run away with you. When this happens, your body begins to regulate itself. You are better able to regulate your emotions and behaviors without as much effort as it would have taken you in the past. You might find that donuts just might not agree with you anymore, without a whole lot of thinking, *I can't eat donuts*. You just decide that you don't want them anymore. The same with alcohol or other substances. You might find that you are not reacting as much, and are more able to respond thoughtfully without the drama.

The reason that these changes become easier is because the process of meditation and a lifestyle of gratitude and mindfulness actually change the brain…and your brain is what runs the show in your body.

Dr. Daniel Amen, author of **Change your Brain, Change your Life**, says, "Decades of research have shown that meditation can calm stress and enhance brain function. Studies have shown that meditation improves attention and planning, reduces depression and anxiety, decreases sleepiness, and protects the brain from the cognitive decline associated with normal aging."

The reason I think that it's important to understand how this happens is that once you understand that this is not just woo-woo, touchy-feely stuff but actually scientifically proven facts, I think you will be more inclined to stick with your practice.

## Chapter 5

# It Does WHAT to My Brain?

We can list benefits from meditation all day long, because it really does affect every area of your life. But let me talk about some things that Rebecca Gladding, MD, has to say as a result of some of the studies she has done. She is the author of **You Are Not Your Brain**. She says that with just 15-30 minutes a day you can start experiencing tremendous changes. Now keep in mind, I am not a doctor or a scientific type, so I am going to attempt to distill some technical information for you into language that even I can understand.

She says that with a regular meditation practice one can begin to notice a change in how you interact with others. If you are one who often gets hurt or offended by what others say, you might notice less reactiveness. It enhances empathy and compassion and gives a general sense of well-being that she even agrees is difficult to describe. This would correspond to what some of you might call a "peace that passes understanding."

**Lateral prefrontal cortex (what she calls in her book, the Assessment Center):** The part of the brain that allows you to look at things from a more rational, logical, and balanced perspective. While helping modulate emotional responses, this part of the brain can help you override automatic behaviors so you can limit the tendency to take things personally. Those knee-jerk reactions that just seem to happen before you can even think about it. This is why I encourage a deep breath before you respond to anything. Meditation and mindfulness will help you stop and do that. This part of the brain can help control the "Me Center."

The technical term for that is the **medial prefrontal cortex**, the part of the brain that refers to you and your personal situation involving your perspective and experiences. It references how you think and how you feel and what you are thinking about as you engage in social activities. It helps you figure out how others are feeling and what they are thinking. It helps you feel empathy. Dr. Gladding calls it the **Self-Referencing Center.**

This section of the brain actually has two sections: one that deals with how you view and interact with people similar to you, and one that deals with people that you see as being different from you.

**The insula** is the part of the brain that Dr. Gladding says "monitors bodily sensations and is involved in experiencing 'gut-level' feelings.... It is also heavily involved in experiencing/feeling empathy."

**The amygdala** is what you might call the stress center of the brain, dealing with fear and anxiety. It's a part of the brain that is responsible for what might be referred to as "knee-jerk" reactions. It triggers the "fight or flight" response when it senses that you are threatened in some way.

She explains that before we start meditating, most people's brains are very strong in connections between the "Me Center" or the medial prefrontal cortex and the fear centers: the insula and the amygdala. For example, it is the insula that focuses on how you are physically feeling so that when you have a headache, you begin to wonder if you have a brain tumor, or if you keep getting stomach upsets, you start looking up online symptoms of stomach cancer. This establishes obsessive thinking or what she calls "repeating loops of thought": Why did he look at me the way he did? I bet he doesn't like me. Maybe he heard a rumor that tells him I'm not a responsible person. I bet he's not going to hire me. You know, the kind of thought loops that keep you up at night.

This is the kind of "mind lock" that I referred to in the last part of the book. That kind of habitual thinking that keeps you stuck and tied down to old habits and reactions.

If the connection with the lateral prefrontal cortex or the assessment center was stronger, it would be easier to view whatever is happening from a more balanced perspective—essentially decreasing the overthinking, ruminating, or mind lock.

So when you begin a regular meditation practice, the neuro-pathways that perpetuate the mind-lock type of thinking begin to weaken. Those connections begin to break down. The quieting of your mind then allows stronger connections to be made between the "Me Center" and the "Assessment Center." You gain a better ability to apply the principles that I talk about in my book, **Peaceful Parenting: 10 Essential Principles**…breathing and detaching. You become better able to step back a bit and become more of a curious observer rather that one who is clearly sucked into the drama and caught up in knee-jerk reactions and habitual patterns. You don't automatically assume that because you have an ache on your side that you are going to die. You don't automatically reach for that unhealthy coping mechanism like food or alcohol because you have created space between your circumstances, your thoughts, and your actions.

You've created a space, however small, to think of alternative behaviors that would serve you better. You open yourself up to new ways of perceiving others and their intentions.

You become more able to ignore worrisome thoughts and patterns of anxious thinking or see them for what they are.

Meditation also enables that part of your brain that focuses on people that you see as different from you to be able to perceive them in another way…to become more compassionate and understanding, rather than reactive and judgmental. You begin to become able to see things from another's perspective even if they have a different thought process or belief system than you. The new neuro-pathway enables you to exhibit more empathy.

Dr. Gladding says that, "In the end, this means that you are able to see yourself and everyone around you from a clearer perspective, while simultaneously being more present, compassionate, and empathetic with people no matter the situation. With time and practice, people do truly become calmer, have a greater capacity for empathy, and find they tend to respond in a more balanced way to things, people, or events in their lives."

One man that has learned these principles, who could only find 5 minutes at a time to meditate, exhibited a remarkable new level of control in certain business situations in which he was unjustly accused of something. Normally, he would have blown up with anger and possibly said and done things that were not in the best interest of his family or his business. (Did you know that your IQ actually goes down when you get angry?) Instead he was able to take a deep breath, separate himself from the false accusation, and leave it squarely in the lap of the accuser. He made some phone calls, asked for legal advice, and prepared a thoughtful response for the accuser and the issue was resolved in a matter of a couple of hours instead of getting all blown out of proportion and creating chaos that might have been very difficult to clean up. And these changes in behavior resulted from the development of his new meditation practice that was only a few weeks old at this time.

Here's where it's very important to continue a regular practice. It's like building a muscle or maintaining a healthy diet. You have to keep doing your exercises or you will lose the strength in those muscles. You could have been a terrific athlete in high school, but you can't continue to live off of those laurels. Because if you were a great football player in high school or college and then just plop on the couch and watch football from then on, you know as well as I do that you will get flabby, no matter how wonderfully enthralling your stories of your glory days are.

The same is true of meditation. It's important to find a way of practicing meditation and a time frame that works for you and keep it up. This doesn't mean you can't change it up from time to time, changing techniques, learning, and growing. It also doesn't mean that you are doomed if you miss a day. But don't let missing a day make you lazy or start condemning yourself. Be gentle, be easy, and relax about it.

And you can see that by maintaining a regular practice it becomes easier to live by the principles I was talking about in the last chapter. You are even learning a few more today.

Here we talked about breathing, detaching, and not judging. So the new one is detaching. You are gaining quite a tool belt of tools and coping skills as you maintain your practice. Here's even some more interesting information.

*The Washington Post* published an article by Brigid Schulte (May 26, 2015) telling a story about Sara Lazar, a neuroscientist at Massachusetts General Hospital and Harvard Medical School. From her own experience with injuries from running, she began doing yoga and found that she began experiencing some changes in her mood and calmness. She found herself to be more empathetic and compassionate and better able to deal with difficult situations, so she started to do research to find out why this actually worked.

She conducted some studies with long-term meditators vs. a control group. What she found was pretty enlightening. She found long-term meditators have an increased amount of gray matter in the insula and sensory regions of the brain, which made sense to her, she said, because when you're mindful, you're paying attention to your breathing, to sounds, to the present moment experience, and shutting cognition down. She says, "It stands to reason your senses would be enhanced."

Her team also discovered more gray matter in the part of the brain associated with working memory and executive decision-making.

Lazar talks about how it's harder to figure things out and remember things as we get older. But in this one region of the prefrontal cortex, the brain looked pretty much the same in the older and younger meditators.

Well, I'll tell you that for me, in my 60s, that's reason enough! I find those results exciting!

Her studies showed that after just 8 weeks of a mindfulness-based stress reduction program, people who meditated regularly and practiced mindfulness principles had positive results that involved 5 different areas of the brain, which brought these results:

1. Mind wandering decreased and focus and positive sense of self increased.
2. Strengthening in ability to learn, cognition, memory, and emotional regulation.
3. Perspective, empathy, and compassion increased.
4. More regulatory neurotransmitters are produced.
5. The amygdala got smaller and resulted in a reduction in stress levels.

As I recommend 20 minutes twice a day, she also recommended 40 minutes a day. But she found that people's practice varied. On average, results showed that the subjects of the studies ended up meditating 27 minutes…some even as few as 10 minutes.

I also have people who are participating in my 90 Day Happiness Challenge who have told me they do about 5 minutes at a time and are experiencing good results. Even though Ms. Lazar commented that further research was necessary, I think what we have heard is pretty compelling and a great place to start!

There have been many different kinds of studies. Eileen Luders, a researcher in the Department of Neurology at the University of California Los Angeles School of Medicine, looks for evidence that meditation changes the physical structure of the brain.

In an article posted by *UCLA Newsroom* by Mark Wheeler (March 14, 2012) we find that everything we do changes the brain.

Of course if you focus on math or learning a language, you get better at math or a language and strengthen that part of your brain. If you focus on music, you get better at music...what you exercise gets stronger; it just makes good common sense.

Luders and her colleagues compared the brains of 22 meditators and 22 age-matched non-meditators and found that the meditators (who practiced a wide range of traditions and had between five and 46 years of meditation experience) had more gray matter in regions of the brain that are important for attention, emotional regulation, and mental flexibility.

She explains that increased gray matter typically makes an area of the brain more efficient or powerful at processing information.

In an article in the **Yoga Journal** by Kelly McGonigal, she states, "Over the past decade, researchers have found that if you practice focusing attention on your breath or a mantra, the brain will restructure itself to make concentration easier. If you practice calm acceptance during meditation, you will develop a brain that is more resilient to stress. And if you meditate while cultivating feelings of love and compassion, your brain will develop in such a way that you spontaneously feel more connected to others."

Now, GRATITUDE can also change the brain for the same reasons. What you focus on expands. I found several different studies about this. One was where some of the subjects were told to write a gratitude journal, remembering things they were grateful for each day. The other group was told to keep a journal about why they were better than others. Another group was told to keep track of things that irritated them over the course of several weeks. The results were that the gratitude group showed greater increases in determination, attention, enthusiasm, and energy. Not only did it improve in these areas, but also they saw an increase in their exercise patterns.

Even more interesting is that there have been studies done to show that your brain actually changes by living a grateful lifestyle. The studies involve those with anxiety and depression. While it was found that gratitude did not directly alter the brain for those with anxiety, it helped them sleep better, and then what followed was that they became more relaxed because they slept better! So gratitude had an indirect impact on those with anxiety, but a direct impact on depression scores.

Either way, with gratitude you're better off, and you get a good night's sleep.

National Institutes of Health (NIH) conducted a study examining blood flow in various brain regions while the subjects were instructed to be in a state of gratitude. They found that subjects who showed more gratitude overall had higher levels of activity in the hypothalamus, which is where hormones are produced. These hormones apparently regulate things like thirst, hunger, sleep, circadian rhythm, moods, sex drive, and the release of other hormones in the body. With these results in mind, it makes sense, then, that we can be more relaxed, sleep better, eat healthier, and have better sex drive and just be less moody!

Also found was that gratitude directly activated brain regions associated with the release of dopamine. Dopamine makes you feel good, and when you feel good, you want to do the thing again that you just did, so it creates better motivation ("The Grateful Brain," Alex Korb, PhD, November 11, 2012).

So here we have studies that prove meditation, mindful behavior, and gratitude actually do change your brain. Keep in mind, though, that it is like a muscle that needs constant reinforcement. You don't all of a sudden become happy and sit in bliss for the rest of your life.

You don't all of a sudden become spiritual and can rest on your laurels as a spiritual guru.

These things create a calm and joyful lifestyle. It does become easier the more you do it, but you have to do it. If you fall off the wagon, so to speak, just hop back on at the next opportunity. Resist self-condemnation.

That principle of non-judgment applies to thoughts about you as well. As a matter of fact, all the healthy principles we are learning begin with you. Because you can't share what you don't have, and sharing is the best way to increase your supply.

Go figure!

# Part 3

# Developing a New Way of Thinking

## Chapter 6

# Dropping Unhealthy Beliefs

I hope things are going smoothly with your meditation practice, your attempts at being mindful and grateful.

As you learned in the last section, if you are establishing a regular mindful/meditation practice there are already changes taking place in your brain. The changes in the brain make it easier for more changes to happen. Chances are, you are becoming calmer, better at decision-making, less reactive, healthier, better in control of your diet and exercise, and more compassionate.

Of course if you are just starting out with this new lifestyle, you may not be seeing significant changes yet. But if you watch closely and become very aware of your responses and feelings and reactions, you will notice small changes. It helps to write down the positive movement that you see and that helps reinforce what you are doing and where you are headed. Our brains do seem to be wired to see the negative, so it's very important to reinforce the positive. And remember that the studies generally noted that they measured results and saw changes after 8 weeks. Even though many have seen results sooner, I want to encourage you to hang in there. Everyone is different.

Remember that we learned that the dopamine being released encourages more positive changes. That should encourage you to keep up the good work.

Now that you have begun to lay the groundwork for change, you might notice specific thoughts or behaviors that seem to just not want to go away. They feel like they have become a part of you, making it easy to fall into the same behavior rut and more difficult to change.

Don't get discouraged. Just know, that while it's not a panacea, the meditation is preparing the ground for change. It is loosening up the ground for new vegetation to break through. Even so, sometimes a pocketful of tools comes in really handy.

One procedure I practice with many of my clients is to help them break through limiting beliefs. In my experience I find that about 90-95% of our issues come from beliefs that we form in childhood. Limiting beliefs that keep us stuck in a rut, bumping into the same wounds over and over again; getting involved with the same kinds of dysfunctional relationships; poor communication patterns; unhealthy ways of dealing with stress. We often learn these things when we are very young…often under 6.

We never approach the process of healing by looking for someone or something to hang the blame on. However, it is helpful to recognize where the unhealthy patterns come from in order to change them. So here are a couple of specific things in addition to meditation, mindfulness, and gratitude that can help you.

**First, let's go over the effectiveness of affirmations.** I know there is some skepticism about the efficacy of affirmations and positive thinking. But I want to affirm to you that studies have also been done on how affirmations can change your brain patterns and change your life.

The reason is pretty simple. Just as we learned in the last chapter, what you focus on increases. And so often, our brains fall into negative default mode. You know how it is when you get 100 compliments in one day, but then you get one negative comment. What is it that your brain glues itself to?

You got it! That one negative comment. And if you allow it, that's what you will focus on and ruminate about. And even though you had a very successful day, you will end up feeling down just because of that one negative. So that just shows us how important it is to be mindful in controlling our thoughts. We have to stay conscious about what's going on in our minds because what goes on in our minds is going to affect your feelings, your behaviors, and thus, your relationships, not to mention, your physical health.

Apparently, the reason we focus on the negative is because a negative event poses some kind of perceived danger. So our brain becomes hyper-focused on how to keep ourselves safe. You become so focused, then, on the negative and all its implications that you become unable to hear or think anything else. Your brain automatically filters it out as irrelevant or unimportant in comparison to keeping yourself safe.

Here's a little experiment. Just take a moment to relax. Go ahead.

Now picture yourself walking in the woods, enjoying the bits of glittering sunshine between the branches. You feel its warmth on your face and the gentle breeze brushing your face and playing with your hair...the beautifully colored leaves or flowers are amazing. You find yourself enjoying the fragrances and listening to the twittering of the birds. Feel it. Picture it. Really tune yourself in.

Suddenly, several feet ahead of you a mama bear appears out of nowhere! What happens to your heart? Your brain? Are you still focused on the sunlight rippling through the woods? Are you still enjoying the fragrances? Probably not. Your focus switches. Your heart starts pounding; all you can think of is, crap, how can I get out of here? What should I do?

Interestingly, the same thing happens when you have a new hairstyle and throughout the day everyone says, "You got your hair cut! Cute! Love it. Very flattering. Youthful…what fun…."

And then one person comes along and says, "Hmm, why'd you get your hair cut? I really liked it better the other way."

Big danger? Little danger? No danger at all? Doesn't really matter…you experience a **brain switch!** All of a sudden you feel the need to protect yourself and our self-preservation takes over everything else.

So what can we do about that?

All it takes is detaching enough to see what's really going on. Just take a breath and step back as soon as you get that familiar feeling…the one that feels deflating or devaluing or afraid, and ask yourself, "Am I really in danger because someone isn't crazy about my hairstyle? What can I do about that?"

1. You can affirm that you really like it, or tell yourself it will grow back; you can remind yourself that everyone else seemed to like it; you can place it in its proper place of relative importance.
2. Now if you really ARE in danger, that quick breath and assessment that says, "Yessir, it's really a bear! I need to get out of here," give you

*Dropping Unhealthy Beliefs*

a moment to figure out the best and most effective escape route.

Dr. Mona Lisa Schultz, MD, PhD, says, "We can rewire the patterns in our brain with cognitive behavioral therapy or affirmations. Affirmations change the way our brains are wired and the brain lights up differently. It really has bio-chemical, neuro-chemical, neuropharmacological effects just as effective, if not more effective, than Prozac, Zoloft, whatever else you have."

Remember this is not magic, but it's not just a Band-Aid either. You actually have to apply the principles regularly and let them seep into your subconscious. We are not just "dressing up a lie"; we are actually digging deep down into our inner truth and our real self, the self that is connected to God, or the universal energy where your core value is planted and firm and unchanging. Sometimes we might lose sight of it, but we are never completely disconnected from it, because we are never disconnected from our Source. There is always a pilot light glowing deep down in there. Sometimes we just need to add the gas, which is your faith and focus.

With the constant application of truth, ultimately something will click and, at some point you will turn the corner. You will no longer feel like you are faking it or putting lipstick on a pig; you will begin to get the revelation that truth is becoming your reality and the false evidence that only appears real is fading. Remember the antithesis of love is FEAR and that is the False Evidence Appearing Real. And you will find that fear fading. You will discover that there never was a "pig" to put lipstick on.

**To be most effective, affirmations must be true, stated in a positive way, and stated in the present tense.**

Your imagination doesn't know if what it is thinking of is actually happening in the physical world or not... and it doesn't really care. What is in there WILL become reality if you allow yourself to verbalize it, think it, write it down, act it out...the more senses you use to learn something the more effectively it will take root.

So make a **brain switch.** Stop the self-talk that says I am a victim. And make a conscious effort to override your subconscious beliefs.

It may even help for you to visualize that you are leaving this plane of what you have always considered "reality" and step into another plane where you make the rules. Step into the plane of quantum mechanics... the plane of possibilities where ANYthing is possible. Imagine you are stepping into the wardrobe with the children who enter into the whole new world of Narnia; follow the characters down the rabbit hole into Wonderland; create a hologram of yourself in the midst of the universe...whatever visualization works for you. But step into a new reality because the one you have been in is keeping you stuck. And the truth is you are NOT stuck, you are free. Your brain is just telling you that you are stuck.

I am a victor; I am in control of my feelings. I am one with love; I am one with the creator. I am also a creator; I have a job that fulfills me; I have a well-functioning relationship with my boss; I am worthy of respect.

NOW take a few minutes and make a list of affirmations that will begin to change your personal situation. Grab paper and a pencil and make your list. Remember, they all start with I; they are in the present tense, and they are based on the truth of your true self, the self that is one with the creator.

The whole point of affirmations is to ultimately change your focus from falsehood to truth. Most of our fundamental beliefs were formed early in our childhoods. The ones that make us feel neglected, unloved, entitled, unworthy, incapable, overwhelmed, or victimized.

When a belief is cemented into our cells with a strong emotional component, it seems to become our "truth," creating opportunity for more similar situations to be drawn to us by our beliefs making those unhealthy thoughts stronger. That's why we seem to find ourselves in the same situations over and over again.

If we had a disapproving parent, we will tend to subconsciously seek out people who disapprove of us. If we had unstable relationships, we will subconsciously seek out unstable relationships. If you believe that there is something wrong with you and people leave you, interestingly enough you will find relationships ending prematurely.

If, for example, when you were a kid and you felt like nobody cared or was watching you, you just took whatever you wanted or bullied other children because you felt bullied, those patterns will tend to repeat themselves as you grow...subconsciously.

Now that may sound like bad news. It might sound like you are destined to be a certain way. It might sound like you have no control over what happens.

The truth is, however, that you *do* have control.

# Chapter 7

# Yes, You DO Have Control

You always have. Just like Glinda, the good witch of the North in the **Wizard of Oz**, says, "You've always had the power, my dear." You just haven't been aware of it. We are creating our own reality all the time. Let's try not to focus on what is "good" or "bad" but let's focus on "what is" without judgment. Once we add judgment to the equation, we get stuck in a certain way of thinking and feeling.

Just let your mind float in the NOW, coming and going like waves. You can acknowledge them and let them go. As soon as you start judging how you feel, you have begun to dig a trench there.

"I am angry…that person is a jerk…why does he always do that? He never cares about how I feel and doesn't listen to what I say…Ugh! I just have to get away from him…he makes me want to scream!" You have followed that feeling down the rabbit hole and you just create more of the same.

Another way to deal with the same situation is to recognize your anger.

I am angry...but that makes me feel crappy...what can I do to feel better? I don't want him to pull me into his reality; I choose to create my own. So I will just leave him to his old patterns of relating and I am going to focus on what makes me happy.

In the second scenario, you determine that you have control and can take that situation in any direction you want, let the anger roll over you, and you then move forward in a powerful way.

In the first scenario, you totally give that other person control over the way you feel. You bite onto it like a pit bull and shake your head and insist on harboring the negativity. You become stuck in a dysfunctional, unhealthy, non-productive pattern and waste your fabulously powerful creative energy feeling like crap!

Examples that I hear from clients about where they feel stuck are mostly in relationships: with a mother, with a child (of varying ages), with a boss, with a sibling, with a spouse. In another situation someone was stuck in a long-held fear...a fear that simply manifested in a new way. These difficulties in relationships are often confounded by other places you feel stuck, such as in an addiction or in a compulsive thought process. Sometimes it's an addiction to porn or alcohol, or even a negative thought pattern. Yes, you can be addicted to thoughts and feelings as well.

Remember, none of these situations is bad. They just are. When you can stop judging it and just embrace it for what it is...recognize it, name it, and determine what you can do about it. And of course once you start looking at it this way, the possibilities are endless. There doesn't have to be a right way of dealing with it or a wrong way... just a list of possibilities: option 1, option 2, option 3. If one doesn't give you the result you want, move on to the next. The whole point is that with this way of looking at things you are the driver, rather than the circumstances.

Of course you cannot make another person feel a certain way or act a certain way, but that has never been your job anyway. Not even as a parent. Your job as a parent is to develop yourself into the most healthy and productive person you can be, creating an atmosphere in your home where your child is free to do the same. When they grow up, they may or may not choose the way you would have chosen for them, but that is not your concern. Your concern is that you have taught them to think for themselves and grow in their true identity, which you are also doing by your example. Kids learn more from your example than they will ever learn from your words or demands.

You do not know the future and what will come of the seeds you have planted. It is just your job to plant healthy seeds to the best of your current ability, which will change as you grow.

When you are stuck in a certain relational pattern, there are certain things that you must do.

**1. Recognize that you are trapped in your current way of thinking/feeling.** We become addicted to feeling a certain way just as we can become addicted to drugs or alcohol. We can become addicted to gambling, to sex, to pornography. And we can also become addicted to anger, helplessness, victimization, being the fixer, being the scapegoat, being disregarded or invalidated. We can become addicted to being "in love," or any feeling at all.

Remember that we learned in the last section of the book that dopamine is released from the hypothalamus, creating that feel-good feeling. As a matter of fact, studies have been done showing that many different kinds of chemicals are released from the brain…there is a chemical for every mood…and just as you can get addicted to drugs, you can get addicted to moods and feelings...the more of whatever chemical is being released, the less you need to feed your addiction. So as I understand it, it takes less and less to create the feeling such as anger, love, hate, joy.

And you can choose to reverse this process at any time by rejecting that feeling and feeding into something else. Or you can stay stuck in the pattern by unconsciously feeding into the feeling with subconscious reactivity. This is why the first step of RECOGNIZING what's going on is so important. If you can't recognize it, you can't move onto step 2, which will begin the change.

2. **Name it**. Acknowledge that you are trapped in a specific pattern that you can name. Anger, being in love, playing the victim, needing to feel appreciated, child, scapegoat, fear: of going out, of flying, or anything else. You can't change anything until you first know where you are and where you want to go. If you want to know how to get to Los Angeles, it's crazy to think that you can get directions if you don't know where you are. You won't know the first turn to make or which road to take. Are you in Cleveland? Mexico City? Washington, DC, or London?

Just as unproductive is identifying where you are: I am depressed, without knowing where you want to end up. If you keep saying I am depressed; I don't want to be depressed; I wish I wasn't depressed; Oh man, I feel depressed; I really want to stop being depressed...what is the one thing you keep reaffirming? Right! Depression.

So in order to get out of that rut, you need to also name where you want to go. **I want to go to Joy and Love and Peace**...OK. Where are you? Cleveland? Want to be out of Cleveland? You have to know where you want to go. Los Angeles? OK...now we can make a plan.

3. **Determine what YOU can do** to get there. What resources do you need? A car? A plane? A bicycle? A map? Gas? Knowledge of how to drive? A plan?

Don't wait until somebody decides to give you a car or don't wait for someone to draw you a map or fill up your tank...YOU figure out how you can acquire a car; YOU go buy a map or look it up online; YOU take driving lessons; You go to the gas station of your choice and fill up your vehicle. Don't wait for the weather to change; don't wait for someone to volunteer; YOU go do it. Then follow the map you've laid out and the end result becomes more assured.

Recognize, Name, Take action.

Part of that plan may be saying affirmations every day, writing them on your mirror, on your steering wheel, as a screensaver on your computer. Say them to yourself; say them out loud.

If we allow our thoughts to continue subconsciously bombarding us unchecked, they can become obsessive and take on a life of their own. One young man learned that he had control over those obsessive thoughts. Here's his story.

> "I had struggled with my OCD since I was a child. It always felt like there was something different going through my head than with others. While working with Marianne I was able to understand my overthinking and my obsessions. Using positive reinforcement and replacing my negative and obsessive thoughts with positive and healthy thoughts, I was able to clear my head one day at a time, until my OCD thoughts almost stopped all together. Now I can think clearly and act with greater confidence, remembering to stay focused on being positive. I am thankful

*for my therapist, Marianne, and this method, which works 100%. I am proof.*

Here is another very powerful way to change your beliefs...I use this technique in therapy often. Sometimes with more deep-rooted issues it works better to have a professional help you through this, but much of it you can do yourself.

As you may know, I practice holistic psychotherapy. I combine the emotional with the physical and the spiritual because you are a three-part being...you are not one-dimensional. So healing must take place in all the parts of you. But you can begin anywhere. You can begin with the spiritual, or the emotional, or the physical, or combine them altogether as I do in this exercise.

Remember that the more specific you are with what you want to change, the more effective change will be... and the more lasting.

Sometimes, people are more aware of their emotions—anger, offense, hurt, sadness, grief, hatred, irritation—so that might be a good place to start.

But in other cases, I find that people really have a difficult time with their feelings but might be very aware of their physical aches and pains (these are generally because we have denied our feelings). So perhaps you have a pain in your lower back, or a frozen shoulder, or headaches, or upset stomach.

Either way, whether it's your feeling or a physical manifestation, the first thing you do is focus on it.

Let me first explain the procedure. Then when you have a moment alone with no distractions, try it yourself.

First, focus on the negative feeling. Turn up the intensity of it. Really feel the anger or pain.

Recognize where you feel that feeling in your physical body. Focus on the part of your body that is uncomfortable: the nausea, the stiff joint, the dry throat, the pounding heart, or whatever it is.

Then simply allow your spirit to drift you back to the first time you felt that way. Stay out of your head. Don't edit; don't try to figure out how it fits together; don't explain it away.

Don't think it through too much, don't evaluate, criticize, or judge. Just go with the flow even if it doesn't make any sense.

Let it lead you back as far in your memory as it can. You are looking for the earliest time you felt this.

When you get to a memory, focus on that memory intensely, feel the feelings; experience the experiences; it was probably as a young child. Feel the fear, the sadness, the disappointment, the pain.

What was it that child believed at the time? I am helpless? I am unloved? I am not important? Nobody cares about me? I am being abandoned? There's something wrong with me? Identify the belief that felt truest at that time. (Resist the urge to nullify it by saying it's not true now or that person who hurt you didn't mean it...I just want you to experience the belief as you felt it at the time.)

Turn up the intensity of the pain and then invite the loving, benevolent spirit that led you back there to reveal to you the truth in place of the wrong or unhealthy belief.

Sit quietly and just observe. Become open to all your senses, so the spirit is free to manifest the truth in whatever way it chooses: through a vision, through a thought, through an emotional release, through a physical feeling. You might feel wrapped in a warm blanket; perhaps someone looked into your eyes with compassion; or do you maybe hear a message in your mind?

When you have received the truth and you feel the release of the negative feeling, just rest in that. Marinate in it, and when you feel finished, open your eyes.

When you change a belief back there in your memory, the trickle-down effect can be very powerful. I have had people suddenly not feel angry anymore, or had a physical pain disappear or get better. I have witnessed people release lies that they are unworthy to be loved, which keeps them from allowing themselves to feel vulnerable with a partner, as well as many other feelings of release.

Do the exercise; you might want to record the following section in your own voice so you can just relax through the exercise.

> So let's give this a try. If you feel stuck in a certain feeling, or physical pain, I want you to name it. Identify it. Give yourself a moment to determine what we will focus on.
>
> First, focus on the negative feeling. Turn up the intensity of it. Really feel the anger, hurt, or pain.
>
> Recognize where you feel that feeling in your physical body. Focus on the part of your body that is uncomfortable: the nausea, the stiff joint, the dry throat, pounding heart, or whatever it is.
>
> Then simply allow your spirit to drift you back to the first time you felt the feeling or emotion. Stay out of your head.
>
> Don't think it through too much, don't evaluate, criticize, or judge. Just go with the flow even if it doesn't make any sense.
>
> Let it lead you back as far in your memory as it can. You are looking for the earliest time you felt this.
>
> When you arrive at a memory, focus on that memory intensely, feel the feelings; experience the

*experiences, probably it was as a young child. Feel the fear, the sadness, the disappointment, the pain.*

*What was it that child believed at the time? I am helpless? I am unloved? I am not important? Nobody cares about me? I am being abandoned? There's something wrong with me? Identify the belief that felt truest at that time. (Resist the urge to nullify it by saying it's not true now or that person who hurt you didn't mean it...I just want you to experience the belief as it felt at the time.)*

*Turn up the intensity of it and the pain and then invite the loving, benevolent spirit that led you back there to reveal to you the truth in place of the wrong or unhealthy belief.*

*Sit quietly and just observe...become open to all your senses...so the spirit is free to manifest the truth in whatever way it chooses: through a vision, through a thought, through an emotional release, through a physical feeling. You might feel wrapped in a warm blanket. Perhaps someone looks into your eyes with compassion, or maybe you hear a message in your mind.*

*When you have received the truth and you feel the release of the negative feeling, just rest in that. Marinate in it, and when you feel finished, open your eyes.*

If you received a truth or a different healthier thought or belief, write it down. You may even want to make a note about how it transpired. You can use this technique any time that you have a negative reaction from which you want to get unstuck. Recognize first that the other person or situation is not the problem. The problem is that you are hooking into a negative reaction.

The good news is you can change it—not by changing your spouse, but by changing your belief.

So in this part of the book, we've addressed three different techniques for changing your thoughts and beliefs.

1. Affirmations
2. Recognition, Naming, and Taking action technique
3. Changing beliefs at their place of origin

Practice these throughout the weeks that follow. Be gentle with yourself. It may not happen in a big revelation, but a little bit at a time. Either way, you are moving in the right direction.

In the next chapter, I will give you specific grounding techniques and a variety of mindfulness practices the you can use anywhere to bring you back into this present moment and all the love and joy and peace and abundance that is present even now.

# Part 4

# Mindfulness and Grounding Techniques

# Chapter 8

# Getting Set Free

One of the participants in the Un-Leashed Life tele-class experienced such a healing experience through the procedure outlined in the last chapter that I asked if I could share it.

> She said, "The visualization of hurts going back to childhood was so easy for me to get to after all the amazing therapy and guidance I have had through you helping me realize where this anxiety was really given its roots. I was able to go back to that little 'Sally' who was so scared and just needed a little extra TLC, encouragement, and reassurance. My mom did not have the patience, time, or empathy to see that. So I went back to that little girl sitting on the stairs at my home soooo scared to go to preschool begging and sobbing, with her soul pleading, 'I can't go, I can't.'
> 
> "The anxiety grew and grew and all I was told was, 'You are going NOW!'
> 
> This led to me feeling extreme anxiety, crying, fear, insecure, abandoned, alone. I spent half the class

> time recovering from the adrenaline searing thru my body. This happened every day!!!
>
> "In the visualization, I saw Jesus come walking toward me at my home and hold out his hands. He lifted me into a big hug and actually carried my small body to preschool telling me, 'I am here; you are safe; I am always here; you are just fine.' He went into the classroom with me and stood at the back of the class and when I looked to him, he smiled and said, 'I am here.'
>
> "Whew that was so vivid!!!! I am taking him with me into a scary appointment I have tomorrow!
>
> "Thank you, that was just what I needed!"

That's powerful stuff right there. So if you haven't experienced a complete breakthrough yet, keep up the work. Keep chipping away at your stuck place!

The exercise that helps you change your beliefs from childhood is very powerful and can be used any time you feel a negative feeling, particularly a recurring negative feeling that would indicate that you are stuck in a certain way of responding. That almost always indicates that that pattern was initiated in childhood because it's deeply rooted in your cells.

So if you need specific help in an area and are having trouble getting unstuck, please see a professional therapist. This book is not intended to replace personal therapy.

Now, having said that, things happen throughout the day (can I safely say, "every day?") that trigger you, hurt your feelings, causing judgmental thoughts. Things arise that irritate you, anger you, offend you, and disgust you. Maybe you feel hateful or nauseous, overwhelmed, panicky, or some other feeling that you'd rather not be experiencing.

So next I will address specific ways to help you to get grounded and feel more secure when you are feeling overwhelmed, indecisive, pressured, and so forth.

You may also need grounding exercise if you have been traumatized and are experiencing flashbacks and/or painful memories. You can use grounding exercises to resist addictive urges to eat, drink, act out sexually, gamble, etc. The next chapter is all about that.

## Chapter 9

# Getting Grounded

Here is a list of suggestions for you to use anytime and anywhere that will help you come back to this present moment. When you feel caught up in a whirlwind of pressure, stress, or emotion, these little exercises can help you be in the eye of the storm, allowing the chaos to whip up around you while you remain centered and calm and present.

- Slowly, silently count your breaths, breathing in for a count of 4, hold for a count of 4, out for a count of 8. Do this ten times.
- Ground yourself by reminding yourself who you are, where you are, and what time or date it is.
- Excuse yourself from the stressful situation for a moment to splash water on your face or get a sip of water. It's helpful to always keep a bottle of water handy. Water helps wash toxins out of your body. So does breathing, by the way.
- If you are outside, feel the breeze on your face. Focus on that for a few seconds.

- If you are standing and there is a desk or chair handy, just hold onto that for a few minutes, feeling the fabric or wood or metal.
- If you are sitting, put both feet flat on the floor and imagine roots growing out from your feet.
- Focus on sounds you can hear inside or outside. Birds, wind, rain, fan, sound machine, music, people talking in another room, heater, fire crackling in the fireplace.
- If you have a drink in your hands, wrap both hands around it, feeling the coolness or the heat.
- Silently name objects that you see.
- Take a walk, feeling each deliberate step.
- Wiggle your toes in your shoes.
- Place your hands in your lap, palms up, and notice the prickly feel of the blood flowing through them. Feel their temperature and any other sensations you become aware of.
- Breathe in and out slowly, noticing what you smell.
- Notice what tastes are in your mouth. Perhaps you could pop in a hard candy and focus on what it feels like and tastes like.
- Pet your dog or cat or some other animal.
- Repeat a comforting phrase or affirmation. "I am safe."
- Make lists in your head of categories, colors, types of cars, words that start with a certain letter.

You, of course, can create your own grounding exercise. Anything positive that uses your five senses or focuses on a part of your body. Perhaps even recalling a favorite song or poem. You can even write things down that you want to remember and keep them in a handy place like your purse or pocket or in a file on your computer, whatever works for you.

Grounding exercises are a type of mindfulness exercise. They can be used in the moment, anytime, anywhere: work, in an argument, to deflect an urge, or to combat overwhelm. Remember you can take back control.

## Chapter 10

# Getting Mindful

N ow let's move on to some other mindfulness exercises that you can do daily or occasionally, as you need, to create a lifestyle of awareness and being in the moment. It's a similar concept, but sometimes they include an activity that can't be done when you are sitting at your desk…but they are fun, relaxing, and peaceful.

One of my favorite mindfulness experts is Alfred James, author of the popular mindfulness blog www.pocketmindfulness.com.

Here, he offers some simple mindfulness practices:

1. The first one, of course, as I said before is always my go-to. It's my favorite: easy to access, easy to do. **Mindful Breathing**. Breathe in deeply and slowly, expanding the diaphragm. There are several ways to do this. He suggests a cycle of 6 seconds in and out, in and out, for one minute.

You might also breathe in for a count of 4, hold it for a count of 4 and breathe out for a count of eight.

For reducing physical pain, you just need to keep under 6 breaths a minute, which is easily done by breathing in for 5 and out for 5 at a minimum. If you have pain issues, you might try this and see how it works.

2. **Mindful Observation.** This is done by simply choosing an object in your immediate area, like a flower or a bird or a bee or the clouds or a lit candle and just observe it for 2 minutes. No judgment or critique, just relax into it and enjoy it for what it is in the moment.

3. **Mindful Awareness.** Whatever simple activity you are doing, slow down long enough to really experience it, whether it is opening a door, starting your computer, noticing the smell of food cooking. Let yourself get caught up in gratitude and wonder for how things work and how blessed you are to have a computer, doors that open and shut, food to eat. Pay attention to things that you usually just take for granted; pay attention and express appreciation for those things or those people: the mailman, electricity, hot water in your shower.

4. **Mindful Listening.** Take some time to listen to music with no distractions, using your earphones or a headset. You might even want to pick something you've never heard before and just listen. Do not judge by beat or genre as something you like or don't like. Just float with it and let yourself fully experience it.

5. **Mindful Immersion.** This takes mindful observation one step further. Take whatever task you are working at and completely immerse yourself in it. Don't rush through it just to get it done; appreciate the process: doing the dishes, mopping the floor, making the bed, or folding the laundry. This kind of activity can even become a meditation, and tasks that you have found bothersome or trivial before can become enjoyable. Some of you may have heard of Brother Lawrence, who lived in the 17th century and was well-known after

his death for this kind of practice. It is captured in a little book called **The Practice of the Presence of God**.

Then, there are things I do with my grandchildren or even alone that nurture awareness and mindfulness:

- **Fishing**…without hurry or too many instructions.
- **Catching tadpoles** in a brook, without worry about getting wet or dirty.
- Taking a **mindfulness hike** where there are certain things you are looking for: different kinds of leaves or mushrooms, listening for different kinds of birds, or paying attention to the leaves crunching under your feet.
- You might even try a **grounding walk** or hike, picturing roots shooting out of your feet with each step…this can be fun for kids.
- **Stargazing**, lying on a blanket or lounge chair at night, just watching the stars.
- Playing a game of **finding shapes in the clouds** while lying in the grass.
- Some people find **painting** a relaxing and mindful experience. Stay FAR away from judgment and just let the brush and paint express themselves.
- **Coloring** mandalas or adult coloring books. Resist comparing or thinking about whether or not it's good; just let go and be in the moment.

The whole concept of creating a mindful life is embracing whatever you find in this present moment. Be in that moment fully, without judgment, without wishing you were someplace else or with someone else or in a different situation.

Know that it is not "reality" per se that determines your happiness level, but how you *think* about and *respond* to what you consider "reality."

## Summary

So the principles we are talking about when we do these mindful activities are principles from my book, **Peaceful Parenting: 10 Essential Principles.**

1. Connecting with your Creator
2. Knowing your true identity
3. Nurturing awareness
4. Breathing
5. Respect for all things
6. Gratitude
7. Limit judgments
8. Detach (observe and become curious)

The two principles that I haven't really addressed in this book are particularly important in relationships. They are:

9. Communicate Clearly
10. Forgive quickly

The reason that they are also important in a mindfulness "breaking through to freedom" type course is because if you don't learn to let grievances go, if you don't learn to communicate clearly and effectively what you want and what you need and how you understand what another is saying, you will continue to be stuck in unhealthy, resentful, and sticky relationships that just continue to cause you grief. If you find yourself aggravated, annoyed, and angry, then you continue to be stuck in a cycle that is keeping you tied up and tied down and you cannot break free.

So here you have a list of things you can do that will keep you in the present moment…things that can keep you from getting sucked into drama or addictive behaviors, feelings, or relationships.

You, throughout this book, have learned the essentials for how to identify exactly where you are stuck, why you are stuck, and ways to get unstuck.

You have learned how to develop a lifestyle of mindfulness and meditation that lays the groundwork for freedom, as well as specific techniques to apply when a feeling or behavior seems particularly difficult.

You have learned why this is important and how it can actually change your brain as you establish new patterns and thought processes.

And finally, you have learned a huge pocketful of tools to help you detach, distract, and get yourself unstuck in the moment.

So now that you have a regular meditation practice and gratitude habit to set the stage for mindful living and a pocketful of tools to change your thoughts and beliefs that are no longer working for you, you have everything you need to begin to break free from whatever is keeping you stuck.

*If you need additional help for a particularly stubborn feeling or habit that you might find yourself addicted to, please connect with a professional therapist.*

Here's to a new free, unbounded you, living the abundant life you were created to live!

Made in the USA
Middletown, DE
16 July 2016